THE ILLUSTRATED BOOK OF FUNNY OLD SAYINGS

Everyday Phrases and Their Origins

SALLY MOONEY

THE ILLUSTRATED BOOK OF FUNNY OLD SAYINGS

Everyday Phrases and Their Origins

Contents

Preface

Have you ever wondered about the funny old sayings people use? Why do we say them and how did they become part of the English language?

For a long while now, I've been fascinated by the phrases and sayings that pop out of people's mouths from time to time. The English language is full of them. We hear people say things like, "don't let the cat out of the bag", "it's raining cats and dogs" and "don't look a gift horse in the mouth". We often know what they mean, but do we know their origins, where do they come from?

Over the last few years, I have been writing these sayings down and researching the history behind them. It's been both fun and fascinating to say the least. I always visualise a playful image of the saying itself which makes me chuckle and the origins are truly intriguing. I don't know about you, but I think it would be very sad if these odd little sayings were ever to be forgotten.

So for this reason, I have finally "pulled my socks up" and "taken the bit between my teeth" and have written this little book containing some of my favourite sayings and illustrations. Whilst the origins of some are unequivocal, others are open to interpretation and may have more than one theory as to the history behind them. In these instances, I am sharing what I believe to be the most likely or in some instances the most entertaining.

I hope you'll agree that the illustrations are both charming and delightful. Having made the decision that my own artistic ability was not going to "cut the mustard", I set out to find an illustrator for the task. How fortunate was I to find the talented, Ecaterina Leascenco, who has been able to translate the images in my head onto paper. It was such an enjoyable process working with her and I cannot thank her enough.

Enjoy!

Don't throw the baby out with the bathwater

Meaning be careful that you don't throw away something valuable in a rush to get rid of unnecessary and unwanted items.

The very thought of this today sounds bizarre, but during the 1500's most people only bathed once or twice a year. Even when they did eventually bathe, the entire family would use the same tub of water, beginning with the father, as the most senior family member and ending with the youngest child. By the time the baby was bathed, the water was pretty dirty and murky, to say the least. Not surprisingly, a mother could inadvertently throw her unseen baby out with the bathwater!

It's raining cats and dogs

This common expression is often used to describe heavy, consistent rain.

Back in the 17th century, English homes often had thatched roofs, and as crazy as it sounds, cats and dogs would often sleep in the thatch to keep warm. On days when it poured with torrential rain, they would leap off to find better shelter, giving the impression of "it's raining cats and dogs."

Another theory is that during heavy rainstorms, dead animals and debris would be washed along the roadside ditches. The sight of these dead cats and dogs floating by may well have led to this phrase.

It costs an arm and a leg

This has to be one of my favourite sayings, and it is used to describe something that is considered to be extremely expensive or excessively pricey.

There are a few theories as to where this saying originates, but the one I think is most likely dates back to George Washington's days when there were no cameras. One's image was either sculpted or painted. Some paintings of George Washington showed him standing behind a desk with one arm behind his back, while others showed both legs and both arms.

Prices charged by painters were not based on how many people were to be painted, but on how many limbs were to be painted. Artists know that hands, arms, legs and feet are more challenging to paint; therefore, painting them would cost the buyer more. Hence the expression, "Okay, but it'll cost you an arm and a leg."

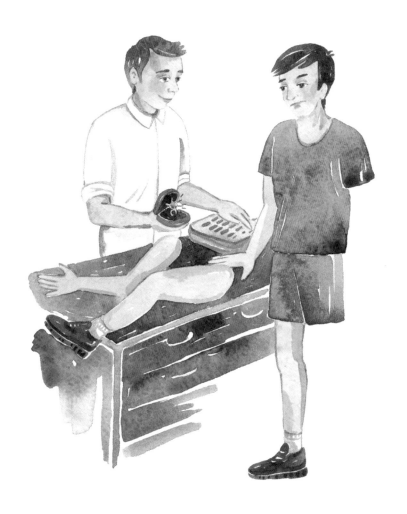

Don't let the cat out of the bag

Meaning don't reveal a secret or disclose some specific information that needs to be kept quiet. It can also be used to refer to someone who is a "blabbermouth."

Back in the 18th century, all sorts of livestock were traded in open-air markets, including pigs. Business people often sold pigs in bags. Some unscrupulous sellers would tell the buyer not to open the bag until they got home, just in case the pig might escape.

The buyer would then carry a wriggling bag all the way home, only to discover upon opening it that they had received a feral cat instead of a piglet. Feral cats were of course, worth far less than a piglet. Needless to say, the cat was let out of the bag, and the swindle revealed leaving the poor unfortunate buyer with nothing to show for his purchase.

Don't look a gift horse in the mouth

An odd little phrase used to remind us about being gracious. It means when you receive a gift or have been offered an excellent opportunity, don't immediately begin to question it or try to find fault with it, but accept it with good grace and gratitude.

In the olden days, particularly in well-to-do circles, horses might have been given as gifts. It was therefore viewed as the height of bad manners, if upon receiving the gift, you looked in the horse's mouth to make sure it had good teeth, was young and healthy and wasn't just an old nag. You see, the length of a horse's teeth is a good indication of how old the horse is as horses' teeth grow as they age.

Bless her cotton socks

A wonderful term of endearment and expression of affection for a child who has done something rather sweet. For example, one might say, "My little niece, bless her cotton socks, picked me a bunch of flowers from the garden."

The origin of this saying dates back to George Edward Lynch Cotton, an English clergyman, missionary, and educator who became the Bishop of Calcutta in 1858. He established schools throughout India for both British and Eurasian children. In his requests back to England for donations of warm clothing, he specifically requested "warm socks" for the children. He held the simple belief that if children had warm socks, many of their problems, such as malnutrition and disease, could easily be solved.

Ladies all over England knitted socks for Bishop Cotton and sent them off to India. As he blessed all items received, many shipments would arrive labelled "Socks for Cotton's blessing" and "Cotton's socks for blessing." Hence the term to "bless one's cotton socks," still remains in use today.

I'll be there with bells on

This means someone is eager and ready to participate. The phrase is frequently used in reply to a party invitation; one might say, 'I'll be there with bells on," meaning they wouldn't miss it for the world, they are excited and can't wait to attend.

It dates back to the days of peddlers when they roamed the area west of the Appalachians in the 1700s selling their wares. To avoid conflicts with the Indians, they travelled as silently as possible until they reached a settled area. Then they unmuffled the bells hung around their horses' necks to announce their arrival to the outlying cabins. Hence, "I'll be there with bells on."

The arrival of the peddlers was a much anticipated major event in the dull and tough lives of settlers. They were not only eager and excited to see the goods that were being sold, but also for the news, letters and messages they carried from the outside world.

Sleep tight

We often hear parents say to their children when putting them to bed, "night, night, sleep tight." It means to have a good sleep, sleep well.

It is thought to date back to Shakespeare's time when mattresses were secured onto bed frames by ropes. To make the bed firmer and more comfortable for sleeping, one had to pull the ropes to make the mattress as tight as possible.

Big wig

Today we use the term "big wig" to describe someone who appears to be, or is, very powerful and wealthy. CEO's and CFO's of large companies are often referred to as the "big wigs."

As incredible as it sounds, men and women took baths only twice a year. Head lice and bugs were a common problem, and while women kept their hair covered, men shaved their heads and wore wigs.

Wealthy men could afford good wigs made from wool. They couldn't wash the wigs, so to clean them, they would carve out a loaf of bread, place the wig in the shell and bake it for thirty minutes. The heat would make the wig big and fluffy, hence the term "big wig."

The pot calling the kettle black

A common little phrase used to describe someone who accuses someone else of having faults or flaws that they themselves have.

It dates back to the early 1600s when typically, most pots were made from heavy materials such as cast iron. Cast iron can often turn black over time as it collects oil, food residue and smoke from being heated over a flame. The story goes that the pot sees its reflection in the kettle's polished surface next to it in the kitchen and erroneously assumes that the kettle is dirty and black too.

Bee in your bonnet

This little phrase is used to describe someone who is fixated on something and cannot talk or think about anything else.

The phrase was first cited in the late 18th century, and its origin is presumed to have been Scottish as bonnets were still being worn there by men, women and children, but had long gone out of use in England. It's not hard to imagine how one would feel if they had a bee in their bonnet or even just a bee buzzing around their head. It would certainly be impossible to focus on anything else.

Born with a silver spoon in his mouth

The idea of this is quite bizarre, as no-one could actually be born with a silver spoon in their mouth! This idiom is used to describe someone who has come from a very privileged or wealthy family. It implies that the person has been lucky and that any status, wealth or advantage achieved in life, has been inherited rather than earned.

In early British aristocracy, it was the tradition for wealthy godparents to give their godchildren silver spoons at their christenings. These spoons were then often used to feed the babies, hence the expression "born with a silver spoon in your mouth."

Mutton dressed as lamb

A rather derogatory phrase used to describe an older woman who has dressed up in an attempt to look younger than she really is. Often her choice of clothing, jewellery, and makeup would seem inappropriate for her age.

This phrase was first used in the Journal of Social Gossip that Mrs. Frances Calvert compiled in 1811 when writing about a musical evening attended by the then Prince of Wales, later George IV. Apparently, when asked whether he thought a particular girl was pretty, he supposedly answered, "Girl! Girls are not to my taste. I don't like a lamb, but mutton dressed as lamb!"

The word "dressing" is often used to describe the preparation of food to make it tastier or look more attractive. This may have led to this phrase as in those days, it was an economic necessity for a woman to marry while still of childbearing years. So for some, it may have been necessary to dress in a way to make themselves look younger and more attractive to men.

Let sleeping dogs lie

If you tell someone to let sleeping dogs lie, you are warning them not to interfere in a situation that is currently stable or not to talk about problems that have happened in the past. It is best to leave well alone rather than potentially worsen a situation.

It is thought to have derived from the long-standing observation that dogs are often unpredictable when they are suddenly disturbed. The expression may well have started as a warning about the risk of waking a potentially dangerous animal, but later turned metaphorical.

Cat got your tongue

This peculiar saying I'm pleased to say has absolutely nothing to do with cats eating tongues! It is an expression said to a person that is at a loss for words or speechless. It is often asked as a question to children that are unusually quiet. One might ask, "what's wrong, has the cat got your tongue," meaning why are you being so quiet, have you nothing to say?

It is hard to pin down the actual origin of this saying, but one gruesome theory refers to the cat-o'-nine-tails, a whip used by the English Navy for unnecessary brutal floggings. The whip caused so much pain that the victims were often left speechless, and other members of the crew would say in jest to a poor ravaged soul, "Cat got your tongue?"

Don't count your chickens before they hatch

A quaint little saying used to advise someone not to rush headlong into action based upon the expectation of something good happening. For example, it would be risky to buy an expensive item that you can't afford, based on the anticipation of receiving a big bonus at work as it might not eventuate. In the same way, you cannot assume that just because you have twelve eggs, you will get twelve chickens as it is unlikely that all eggs will successfully produce a chick.

This phrase is thought to originate from the Greek fable writer, Aesop, who lived between 620 and 564 BC. In his fable, "The Milkmaid and Her Pail," the milkmaid, while carrying her pail of milk on her head, daydreams of becoming independently wealthy from selling her milk to buy chickens which will all produce eggs. She imagines herself being able to say "no" to all the young, unsuitable men trying to win her heart. In being so caught up in her daydream, she inadvertently shakes her head in saying "no" and drops the bucket of milk, spilling it everywhere and destroying any possibility of fulfilling her dream. There is a line from the fable which reads, "Ah, my child," said the mother, "Do not count your chickens before they are hatched."

Eat humble pie

To eat humble pie means to admit to being wrong about something, whilst maybe feeling a bit humiliated or submissive at the same time. Often it's after someone else has pointed out your error or mistake, forcing you to make an apology.

The origin of this idiom dates back to the middle ages when the lord of the manor would hold a feast after hunting. He and his peers would receive the finest cut of meat at the feast, but those of lower standing would be served a pie filled with the entrails and innards, known as "umbles." Receiving "umble pie" was considered humiliating because it informed others in attendance of the guest's lower status.

Go cold turkey

As opposed to gradually giving something up, this means to abruptly quit doing something which is typically considered bad for you, such as smoking, drugs or alcohol.

The origin of this phrase is a little unclear but was in use during the 1920s when referring to drug withdrawal. People believed that during the initial stages of withdrawal, the skin of a drug addict became translucent, hard to the touch, pale, and covered with goose bumps, almost like the skin of a cold plucked turkey.

Let your hair down

This is a rather light-hearted way of suggesting that someone should go out and have some fun for a change. It means to leave your inhibitions behind and allow yourself to behave more freely than usual.

This phrase dates back to the 18th century when Parisian nobles risked condemnation from their peers if they appeared in public without an elaborate hairdo. Some of the more intricate styles required hours of work, so of course, it was a relaxing ritual for these aristocrats to go home at the end of a long day and let their hair down.

No spring chicken

If you are no spring chicken, then the chances are you are not as young as you used to be! This little saying is used to describe someone who is past his or her prime and can no longer do the things they were once able to do when they were young.

In New England, chicken farmers generally sold chickens in the spring, so the chickens born in the spring yielded better earnings than chickens that survived the winter. Sometimes farmers tried to sell old birds for the price of a new spring chicken. Clever buyers complained that the fowl was "no spring chicken" and so the term came to represent anyone past their prime.

You can't make a silk purse out of a sow's ear

Another odd little saying which means you can't turn something ugly or inferior into something attractive or expensive.

This expression was already a proverb in the mid 1500s. It is an English corruption of the French word "sousier." In old France, the peasants would keep their money in a ratty old purse called a sousier which comes from the old French coin, the sou. The purse would be made of rough, humble cloth used for this very practical purpose. There was no way of making a fine silk purse from a tatty, rough cloth sousier, or even from a sow's ear for that matter!

Posh

Where else other than Britain are the elegant and well to do described as posh. Yes, posh means fashionably luxurious, upmarket and stylish.

The story goes that POSH stands for "Port Out, Starboard Home" and dates back to the old empire days when people travelled between England and India. The most desirable and expensive cabins on the ships were those that faced north, avoiding the heat of the sun. Therefore, the wealthy and more well-to-do passengers that could afford these shady cabins would have both their tickets and baggage marked as POSH.

A bird in the hand is worth two in the bush

This 16th-century proverb warns against taking unnecessary risks and suggests that you should keep what you have and not risk losing it by going after more.

It is better to keep what you have (a bird) than to risk trying for more and ending up with nothing (two birds out of your reach). The other reading of the meaning is that it refers to medieval falconry, where a bird in the hand (the falcon) was a valuable asset and certainly worth more than two in the bush (the prey). It may well be that both of these meanings were intended by the coiners of this proverb, which may go some way to explaining why it has resonated over the centuries and is still in common use today.

Cooking the books

Someone said to be cooking the books is thought to be deliberately distorting a company's financial accounts, often with the aim of avoiding the payment of tax.

Cooking seems a rather odd choice of word to convey fraud. However, the Oxford English Dictionary lists a dozen or so meanings of the verb "to cook." Apart from the obvious one "prepare food by the action of heat," there is also the meaning, "present in a surreptitiously altered form," and it is that meaning of cook that was used in the coinage of the phrase "cook the books."

The allusion appears to be the changing of one thing into another, as in when we add a bunch of ingredients together and cook them, the finished look is very different. The first usage of this phrase dates back to Stuart and possibly Tudor England and was used by the Earl of Strafford in his letters and dispatches, 1636: "The proof was once clear; however, they have cooked it since."

Frog in your throat

The thought of this is somewhat unpleasant, to say the least! The phrase means to have difficulty in speaking because your throat feels dry and you want to cough, or you feel hoarse due to phlegm in the back of your throat.

It is believed that the phrase originated in America and became part of the vernacular in 1894 when it was used in an advertisement as the name of a proprietary medicine for sore throats. The advertisement read, "Frog in your throat, stops that tickle! Greatest Cough and Voice Lozenge on Earth."

Minding your P's and Q's

This is said as a gentle warning to behave in a correct and polite manner. A mother might say to her child "mind your P's and Q's when we are out this afternoon," meaning be courteous and remember to say please and thank you.

It is thought that the origin of this saying can be found in old local taverns, pubs, and bars when people drank from pint and quart-sized containers. A bar maid's job was to keep an eye on the customers and keep the drinks coming. She had to pay close attention and remember who was drinking in "pints" and who was drinking in "quarts," hence the phrase "minding your P's and Q's." Customers were also well advised to watch their P's and Q's to make sure they were not overcharged at the end of the session.

Under the weather

This is a frequently used saying used to describe someone that is feeling sick and unwell.

Like so many phrases, this one has nautical origins. It used to mean that someone was seasick which was usually caused by the boat swaying about in bad weather. In the olden days, if a sailor were seasick, he would be sent down below to help with his recovery, under the deck and away from the weather, hence the phrase "under the weather."

Saved by the bell

This idiom essentially means to be saved or spared from an unwanted situation by the timely intervention of something or someone.

As scary and as gruesome as it sounds, being buried alive was once a common occurrence. People who feared succumbing to such a fate were buried in special coffins that were connected to a bell above ground. At night, the guards listened for any bells in case they had to dig up a living person and save them. They were literally saved by the bell.

White elephant

The expression "white elephant" is used to describe an expensive possession which is troublesome or useless and cannot easily be disposed of. For example, a holiday home that is too run down to sell and yet too costly to upkeep, could be described as a "white elephant."

This expression originated in Thailand, where white elephants were once considered highly sacred creatures and were a symbol of royal power. All those discovered were given to the king. However, according to legend, they were also bestowed as a subtle form of punishment. If a Siamese king became dissatisfied with a subordinate, then he would present the unfortunate man with the gift of a white elephant. While this may have been considered a most generous reward, the cost of keeping the elephant was very expensive indeed, and in most cases drove the recipient into financial ruin. References to this story date back to the early 1600s, and the idiom "white elephant" began to be used in the 1800s.

About Sally Mooney

Living in Sydney, Australia and now retired from the corporate world, Sally has plenty of time for her interests and hobbies. She enjoys being creative and making up games for children, cooking up treats in the kitchen and writing silly poems and little books for family and friends.

Sally was brought up in the South of England and it was not unusual for her to hear funny little sayings pop out of people's mouths. A number of years ago, she developed a fascination for these sayings and started to research their origins. Hence, "The Illustrated Book of Funny Old Sayings" came about. With the encouragement and help from her friend Sam Clarke, this is her first book to be published and hopefully it will not be her last!

Sally and Sam continue to work on other fun projects and have created the "Cooking with Smiles" Facebook page. "Cooking with Smiles" is all about kids having fun while learning to cook. We share photos, videos, recipes, jokes, hot tips and more. Our aim is to encourage children to get involved in the kitchen, learn some basic cooking skills, gain some knowledge about food and healthy eating, and most importantly, have a fun and enjoyable experience.

Follow us on Facebook

https://www.facebook.com/cookingwithsmilesnow/

Smile and the world smiles with you!

Bonus – "Sayings Game"

Thank you so much for purchasing this book!

If you like this book, we would be most grateful if you could help us out by taking a few moments and leaving us an honest review on Amazon. Thank you so much.

As a FREE BONUS for purchasing this book, we would like to gift you a game to play with your family and friends. The game involves taking a card from the pack and guessing what the saying is from the picture. We have had a lot of fun playing this ourselves.

Simply visit this link below and we will email you a pdf of all of the illustrations in the book, plus a couple of new ones for fun, together with instructions on how to play the game.

https://www.sci-pty-ltd.com/bonusgame

First Printing, 2020

Printed in the United States of America

Printed in Germany
by Amazon Distribution
GmbH, Leipzig